Symbols of God's Love

Codes
and
Passwords

By Jeanne S. Fogle

Illustrated by Bea Weidner

The Geneva Press
Philadelphia

PRINTED IN THE UNITED STATES OF AMERICA
2 4 6 8 9 7 5 3

Library of Congress Cataloging-in-Publication Data

Fogle, Jeanne S.
  Symbols of God's love.

  Companion v. to: Signs of God's love.
  SUMMARY: Text and illustrations explain the origins and meaning of such Christian symbols as the cross, lily, boat, butterfly, flame, fish, and lamp.
  1. Christian art and symbolism—Juvenile literature.
[1. Christian art and symbolism] I. Weidner, Bea, ill.
II. Title.
BV150.F63 1986   246′.55   86-12014
ISBN 0-664-24050-X

Published by The Geneva Press®
Philadelphia, Pennsylvania

Why is there a cross on top of our church steeple?

The cross is a symbol that is very important to all Christians.

Symbol? Oh! One of those hard words.
What does THIS one mean?

Symbols are like a code. They can be drawings or letters or pictures that help us understand something without using words. We often see symbols near schools and hospitals or along highways and railroad tracks.

... Like the squiggly one that tells us there is a curve in the highway

. . . And the one at the zoo that reminds us not to stick our fingers in the giraffe's cage

. . . And the one that tells us to stop and get that big ice cream cone—right now!

There ARE symbols everywhere.

Yes. And Christians have used special symbols from the beginning. You will see them in our churches, our homes, and our books. These symbols tell stories of Jesus and the church.

How can a symbol tell a story?

When we look at a symbol, we remember some special part of these wonderful stories of Jesus. Let me show you. We can start at the beginning. There is a special symbol that helps us remember that Jesus was born. We see this symbol at Christmas time.

I know. That's easy! It is a star, isn't it?

That's right. One special star was very bright when Jesus was born.

That must be why we put that symbol
at the very top of our Christmas tree.

And there is a symbol that reminds us
of when Jesus was baptized.
It is a dove.

A dove? How is that a symbol of baptism?

One day Jesus walked down to the Jordan
River and John baptized Jesus in the water.
God sent a dove as a sign that Jesus was
special and belonged to God. God was proud
and pleased about Jesus.

Were you proud of me when I was baptized?

Very proud. We wanted everyone to know that you belonged to us.

We see these symbols inside our church—
a loaf of bread and a cup.

I know about these. Jesus left them
to help us remember that he was here.

You do remember! On Passover night Jesus
had a special meal with the friends he loved
most. They gathered to eat and to pray.

Jesus said, "Every time you eat bread
together and drink from the cup, please
remember me." The loaf of bread and the
cup remind us of what happened that night.
When we see these symbols, Christians
remember how much Jesus loved us.

Now, here is the symbol you saw at the top of our church steeple.

The cross?

The cross reminds us of a very sad time, the day Jesus died on a cross.

But why do we put crosses everywhere if they make people sad?

Looking at the cross does make us sad. But seeing it reminds us of how much God loves us. In fact, God loved us so much that Jesus came to show us how to love one another and to live together in peace. Even when others hurt Jesus, he still loved them and forgave them.

This is a symbol for Easter.

A flower. Why?

This is a special flower, a lily. After it blooms each spring, the blossoms and the leaves wrinkle up and die. You might think that the lily is dead. But the roots are still alive, and the lily bursts into bloom again the very next spring.

16

But what does that have to do with Easter?

Everyone thought Jesus was dead that first Easter morning. Then, just like the lily, Jesus burst out of the tomb. Alleluia! Jesus is *alive!*

Some Christians also use this symbol at Easter.

A butterfly?

Remember the cocoon we saw? We thought the caterpillar died after it went into the cocoon. But it didn't! It broke out of the cocoon as a butterfly and sailed through the air, more beautiful than ever.

The caterpillar is still alive, but in another way, just as Jesus is still alive.

Here is a different symbol.

A funny boat on top of a globe?

Yes. This boat is a symbol for the church in the world. Jesus is the captain, who keeps the church going in good times and in bad times.

The sail looks just like a cross. Do you think the people who chose it knew that?

I think so. Another reminder of the cross.
And the globe reminds Christians of the
very last words Jesus said to his disciples,
"Go and teach all nations and baptize them
in my name." Jesus wants those who love
him to tell everyone in the whole world
about God's love.

Another important symbol
for Christians is the flame.

A warning sign?

No, something very different. After Jesus
had gone to be with God, the disciples felt
lonely and sad. One day they gathered to
celebrate a special holiday called Pentecost.

Then a strange thing happened. The wind
began to blow very hard, and all at once a
fiery light moved around the people. They
began to talk in different languages, but
they understood each other. What can this
mean? they wondered.

Peter said, "I know. This light surely is a
sign from God. We must join together and
spread the good news everywhere."

Is this when the church was started?

Yes. That is why Christians say that Pentecost is the birthday of the church. The symbol of the flame reminds us of that. Those early days in the life of our church were very dangerous for the Christians.

Why was that?

Because some people and their rulers did not understand the Christians and their message of love. The Christians were teased and hurt. Sometimes they were even killed.

That is scary!

Yes, it was scary. The Christians had to keep their places of worship secret. They chose a secret password so that they would recognize one another.

Another symbol?

Yes. A fish.
Christians used the symbol
of the fish as a secret password.

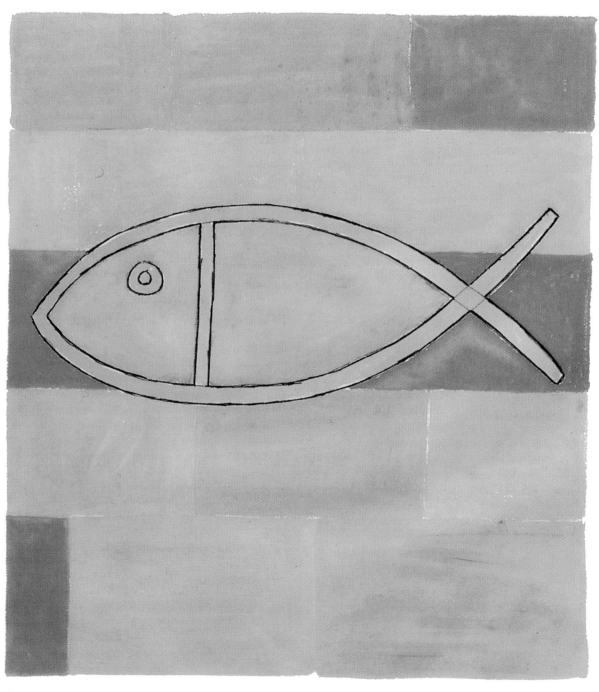

Can we use the password?

Yes, but it is not a secret any longer.

This is another interesting symbol that Christians use. Christians have a special symbol for the Bible, a lamp.

Is that a lamp?

Yes, an old lamp. The lamp is a symbol for understanding. We don't get lost if we can see where we are going. The Bible is like the light from a lamp that helps us to find our way. That is why Christians are called people of the Way.

Symbols do tell stories, don't they?

Yes, and there are many more symbols
that tell stories about our faith.

I am going to watch out for them.

Remember when you see them that they tell us of God's great love.